Emergency Landing

Emergency Landing

A collection of poems and prosaic expressions

Osakwe Kinshasa

OSAKWE KINSHASA: EMERGENCY LANDING

Andrew Burton Publications
P.O. Box 5399
Kingston 6

ISBN 979-864-515-046-4

Cover photograph by Andrew Burton

Book design, cover and typesetting by Andrew Burton
Cover concept by Andrew Burton

Dedicated to JFK

Jennifer – Inspired and saw probabilities.
Fatima – Knows man performs his duty.
Kariamu – Cares and cares not.

Acknowledgements

I thank everyone who reads this collection

You are the main reason I have written it.

I am grateful for the assistance, encouragement and support I got from family, friends and associates while it was being created. The gratitude I have for you will last until I join the ancestors. You are patient and understanding. That is invaluable.

As my innerstanding deepens my gratitude for you grows from joy, harmony, and balanced vibrations. I could not have done this without your support.

Thank you for all you have done and keep doing.

Introduction

Even if it does not say "I love you" it is still a love song. This is my love song to you.

On June 1, 2008 I read some poems at a place named Weekenz on Constant Spring Road, Kingston, Jamaica. When asked how he should present me to the audience, I told the MC to say, "I am a fulltime poet working part time in retail" and that he had the liberty to say anything else he wanted. He said what I had suggested and some very glowing things that I had to live up to for the next thirty or so minutes. His words and my vision of myself were a perfect combination for encouraging a set that the audience loved from the moment I greeted them. I loved their response and gave all I had in me. It was a winning combination that fed into and gave to each other. I had gone there to read publicly for what was supposed to be the last time. I was very wrong about that. The response reminded me this is an innate part of me.

If I knew why after almost thirty years this is the first collection of poems that I am presenting, I would tell you at this point. I do not know why. What I do know is that it feels right, perfect even, to present them now. (Now is all we have.) They explore a range of my emotions, these poems. They make no claim to solve anything. They reflect snapshots of my writer's journey and windows to my evolving positions.

Many of the poems in this small collection were written when I served in the military. Immediately after military service, I went to work in a grocery retail organization and had a good time doing it. People... For what I considered a very a very long time during the retail gig, which began at the cusp of the turn of the century and lasted a few weeks shy of a decade, I wrote few poems. Poetry never left me though.

She stayed with me. As she has done since the early nineties she calms me or agitates encouraging action, but she does not leave. When I reach for her, she pours herself through my fingers, touches gently, strokes reassuringly and kneads where there are gnarly knots, giving ease, relief, and cause for more action. Poetry for me is a release valve, a salve for my inner bruises and a source of expressing thoughts I otherwise may have kept to myself or said at a moment that makes a room go silent or burst into incendiary chatter. Because of her I will never implode or snap. She gives ease to that which irks and creates angst, but she only does it when I reach for her from my heart.

Whether I hid behind a rifle or allowed myself to be boxed in and shelved in an aisle with little traffic near the cold frozen foods, poetry remained with me. The past few months of this great global recalibration gave me a space to put some of these musing in this book. I hope you find value in these pages and find some of these passing thoughts relatable. More than anything, I hope you will write the poetry and prose that have been with you. Let them flow out of your heart onto paper with love.

Table of Contents

A Poem

Poems are just what
they are
Poems…
It's like poem
writing the writer
Poem reads readers
It asks,
what of blank pages,
your ink?
The world is waiting
to hear what I think
of you

Opportunity Knocks

Opportunity knocks
I open
Opportunity challenges
my faith, tests my mettle
The kettle hisses, whistles
The steam, cooler than
burning desire to rise
Trek to mountain top
Opportunity knocks
I open
Opportunity knocks me
down to deep valley
where topsoil is richer
where mountain sets
foundations, gets strength
to stand so tall up where
air is rarefied
Opportunity knocks
I open-minded enough
to make circumstances
for opportunity to walk
right in past gatekeepers,
past doormen, receptionists
right up to penthouse's
easy chairs
Opportunities seek me
the receptive, perceptive
creator of opportunity's
favourite space near
fireplace when outside

is frosty white
Not ever amazed or fazed
by opportunity's demands
I deliver her goods
Opportunity knocks
for me to make opportunities
for others to rise!

Loveable

I am the man you love to love
I am the man you cannot hate

Wait!
I've just overturned the table
At your feet a meal, broken plate
The state of a fear's diminishing
returns will come to an end

I am the man you love to love
I am the man you cannot hate

The slate is clean
"You know what A mean"
Says the African American
A minority group in number
The majority underground,
Underground the subway train
burrows from borough to borough
The smiles (lack thereof), plastic
Plastic Metro-Cards
Plastic credit cards
Borrow to borrow

I am the man you love to love
I am the man you cannot hate

No, you are not offended
Not by pun intended
It was no fun running

from slave chase
Manhattan is a big place
built on my kindred's sweat, tears,
blood
You bet the deck is stacked
So, go ahead deal it, trump croupier
We will make favourable circumstances
See the Black Man dances
on pin's point, razor's edge
Joint by joint problems dissected
challenges erased

I am the man you love to love
I am the man you cannot hate

Lie to yourself if you choose to
Not to me
I see you bothered, see you smart
When I tell you from the heart
orchard, apple cart
All, are my family's
They are the Red Man's
Touch no more, those fruits
There must be some heed to this greed
We, seeds planted, trees nurtured,
fruits harvest
You divest!?!
I think not
That's a truth
Another truth – I rode underground
with Mama Moses, with Tubman
I am conscience

A to Z of Mama Vie

African skies cried from billowy clouds
when she was born captive in Jamaica
She chided backra, challenged the status quo
more daring than Simba's lioness
for her energies come from within where
unhealthy fantasies die young
Her father, my great grandfather
he was a conqueror of men,
of duppies alike
How many the cuts, sores, bruises, she nursed
with herbs of the Manchester plateau
How intense, her love for her offspring
As intense as Jan Hoy's love for Ethiopia
Colours are in the rainbow
All a reflection of her kaleidoscope of hope
A language so colourful
all the canvas in France could never capture
Arch the blue sky where
jets fly but not near her mountains of love
Majesty is for kings and queens, so is wisdom
Common sense for all who acknowledge
there is nothing new in these organic prayers
Freedom for her offspring who are regal
Still...
As still as Imhotep's tomb
Time stood still when Jericho's walls fell
She knows that story
She doesn't know how coltan is extracted
Still, she in valour she waits for the victory
We work, we wait with her patiently

6

Over the years when the excellence shines through
if she is not here we will carry her far
to Congo Zaire, Zambia, Zimbabwe
If she is not here
We will carry her far in memories to
Zanzibar…

Nana Pamela

Beauty queen of Virginia fame
Master of diplomacy game
Give us just one more, only one
Charming smile, reassuring word
Tell us more about Robeson,
Bates, King
Sing Redemption Songs
spirituals of victories, joy, growth
Give one less reason for strong drink
From gin to loom, boutique, showroom
Clothed us regally you did
Weave us messages of hope
Gye Nyame, Sankofa
Scope of advancement
Source of determination
Frustration flees from knowledge
Success walks with courage
Free from self-imposed limits
Upon tight rope high wire
Poised, stoic, gracious, charming
Heart warming
Give us one more,
A smile,
Another reason for songs of joy in
"One Heart" country
It is an epoch-making tour,
Yours
A ray of hope, you gave books,
a compass, map
Can't afford even a nap

Too many journeying on this road
Another well saved penny
adds to that dollar until
we hit mother lode
Light as baby chick's feather
this lead filled load
Just one more smile
Put winds to sail
Tell another tale
Speak, much travelled one
From Virginia to Cape Town,
Bloemfontein, Pretoria
Tell of Madiba
Unyielding faith in humanity's goodness
Unwavering quest for life's utmost
Journey with joy from Kingston's coasts...

Love Grows

Falling in love is not euphoric
Falling invariably hurts
Growing in love is euphoric
Being loved while loving is euphoric
That buttresses roots
With strong roots the
willow withstands
many storms, standing
Standing, growing stronger
in love is euphoric.

Falling in love helps no one

Grapevine

He said
Wine's a mocker
She said
I want to be mocked
shocked by what
I would do under
your influence
unable to escape
this dark grape
I want to be
bewildered by
your grasp
of my desires

Voice I Choose

…then with her
silky smoothness
her voice wraps around me
like warm comforter
on rainy tropical mountain night,
…and when the fiery promise
burns its warm presence
over Mountain Blue
her mysterious
eyes give songs
to my thoughts of gratitude
grateful…
grateful ears
accepts golden honey
smoothness
smoother than oil
pouring all over
my receptive senses
cherished, cherishing
cherish her voice
gentle on delicate anvil
inner ear
soul me
soulful she
we, us, together in songs
this day I cherish
grateful…
Sade Adu my love in songs

Cherished…

Admirer

It is the rhythm of her hips
It causes her skirt hem
to swish right
swish left, right again
That's right
It is the cleavage
The figure
The temptress in her
sensual relevance of
full African lips
that make kisses a great
wish, make wishes bliss
Hi there, Miss…
A moment of conversation
to be acquainted?
I've already painted
a picture of you without
makeup with sunlight
caressing your curtains,
hugging your blinds
at daybreak
Imaginations of your
sheets, pillows approving
I beg your pardon if I
appeared to stare
It's partly what you are
wearing but more
how you wear
Aura, poise, endearing
Presence, personality

You leave a lot to
this man's imagination
I imagine lace
How you soften my
edges harden my core
It's more I ask for
Conversations more
challenging that crosswords
Words warmer than hot wax
Eyelids fluttering like candlelight
Cheeks flush like red wine
Cold nights, warm chocolate
marshmallows melt easily
Strawberries tangy, sweet
Grapevines entwine our minds
We find more ways
to be interested
Time invested passes
like shooting stars
Starry skies, moonlight
Silver rivers into golden age
Cascading memories of the
first moment our eyes met...

K Pods for Smiles

Thanks for the pods
The caffeine makes
differences
especially when
previous night was short
Thanks even more
for your smiles
They bring more
energy than coffee
at its strongest
On days when your
smiles are in short supply
please know
that I have a reserved one
Just for you…

Counting Up

She gave me a seven
for a six
I gave her eight
She said take nine
Quizzically looked I on
No not sixty-nine
That was another time
Done all of that
This is a different time
Not on this vine
We are counting up
Counting on each other
to do especially that which
cannot be counted,
valued, priced
Priceless
Depending on us to
do what's best
For us we have chosen love
We count not what we do
Scores we do not keep
Foibles, flaws, shortcomings
we shorten their supplies
We multiply ways of seeing
what's best in each other
She gave me a seven for a six
I gave her eight
She said take nine

Take time to know yourself
I will help you make the best
of who you are
Patient, gentle kind to you
Treat me well
I will find ways to treat you better
Give of your best
I will match it with all of me
Count on me
I am counting on you

Figured Out

Account ants
Drones' hives, currency mills
Worker bees
please boss, freeze wages
Balance books
Move rook
No move pawn
Yawn for hunger
No, sleep
Deprivation
Yawn
Boredom begets pages
pages, pages, even more pages, yet,
beget slave wages for post-graduates
Sit boy, sit girl minds awaiting Pavlovian bell
Worksheets don't lie
Lie here beside
me on this desk
Too narrow
Floored by instincts
Spreadsheets at home another day
Family can wait
Wait, we are alone here
Night is long with tuneless song
Cubicles are close enough for proximity
for fondness, attraction
Wide enough aquariums, starfish
Lay with me, play with me
I play you
You pay me

I lay with you
You pay me
Nothing personal here
Business is business
I come with the colony
I give account, ant's trail to the bottom
Ants' only quest to be like other ants
Individuality is for thinkers
I have this all figured out
Figures don't lie
Account's ants think not of feelings
We process
This trail is well worn
It leads back to the colony
Colonial legacies stacked higher
than palaces' turrets
Queen's keeping court
We give account
Ants follow known trails in silence
Action oriented
Oriented to act on instructions, rules
Family first after corporation's guidelines
Tightrope balancing act
Maintain balance
We obey the bottom, base instincts
Bottom line has no friends, no family...

...books balanced

Net Worth

Honesty is the best
policy to make one
vulnerable
I'll be as vulnerable
as a fish on
on the end of a line
When I am online
I won't be caught
in the net
It's gross what
I've netted for
my efforts
Still, I won't weave
a complex web
Site of lies

Talk is Not Cheap

Money talks, never cheaply
Money talks, see how it orders me
Money talks, yet it never greets me
Mr. Money he steps with snobbery

See my friend, he knows words aplenty
Many words in his vocabulary
He talked long until his stomach got empty
All he said must have been flattery
No one listens attentively
Now he watches in awe
as money talks softly
Money gets attention quite easily

Money talks, not of pity
Money talks, in the inner-city
Money talks, for the man with plenty
Money talks, at the man who lives in poverty

Most people have wishes, favourite dishes
Have money you may have any dish taste bud savours, relishes
Lack money dishes remain wishes
Doctors refuse to give stitches
Try to be prepared for emergencies
and let your money talk

Money talks, not of sympathy
Money talks, subtle with cruelty
Money talks, people will even kill to get plenty

There is evidence
We see continually coins and notes associated with disparity
Pound pence, dollar cent...
Yen again there is no difference in the currency
Man gets respect based on spending ability
Worldwide they accept a nonsensical argument
that a poor man is a thief, scumbag, low down rotten sort of element
if he takes one red cent
In Jamaica in the nineties
Rich people were called on to blaze through
with workers' money through national commercial banditry
See them come with dictionary, come to confuse us with thesaurus
That act is fraudulent, misappropriation and embezzlement
Kindly sit down, be quite, reverent, and listen to the monologue
This is a one-sided money argument...

Money TALKS!
Work, save, and invest wisely
Money TALKS...

Charged Subliminally

Early
Surely to bed
Rise to behold
with these ears,
these eyes
Eyes filled with tears
So many years
Plantation journeys
Land Ahoy!
Columbus Park?
Morgan's Harbour?
Land Ahoy!
Decoy, enjoy
Land Ahoy!
Subliminal the ploy
Psychological
Terminal velocity
Détente, diplomacy
Early
Surely to bed
Rise to behold
with these ears,
these eyes
ventriloquists ventriloquize
Rise!
How far in chains?
Chains around brains
For generations
Whither Ferdinand?
Whither Isabella?

Whither fella from Genoa?
Land Ahoy!
Stalemate, gridlock
Move, check
Move again, check
Check the chains
maintained by the chained
Land Ahoy! Ahoy! Ahoy!
Ahoy!
Subtle, subtle
Subtle about being subtle
Land Ahoy!
Suave, congenial
Mr. jailer has wrong criminal
Early
Surely to bed
Rise to behold
These ears, these eyes
Long arm of the law
Tentacles
Manacles on screens
that are only seen
with mind's eyes
Another pawn is gone
A life
A statistic?
What's the calibration
of the bullet?
Land Ahoy!
Red man, reservation
Black man
Estate, plantation

Sharecrop, Jim Crow
Division
Incalculable reparations
Early
Surely to bed
Rise to behold
These ears, these eyes
Mr. doesn't feel
Really doesn't know
Can only pretend to empathize
Rise realize this babel
Read these fables
These Cains, these Abels
Box office hits, profits
These choking cables
One-way tickets for gullible
Table's turning
Inevitable...

Dean of the Corps

A lion is a big cat
Saw cat sitting on mat
Diplo matte finished
Glossed over, polished
Ratification is the process
of catching rats in act
of baiting cats
Catastrophe
Atrophied, lack of using,
mind, using intuition,
A trophy for rat
that seeks lion share
for itself alone
My "friend" I put in
quotation marks
I hear dogs bark in vain
at cats too big to
be bitten by the flea ridden
In a world of dog hearted
cannibalizing for sport
my "friend"
I put in quotation marks

Doing Time

I am doing time
Corporate nine to nine
Judge me not by
my appearances
Being booked to appear
Before the mirror
I looked beyond
where Garvey had led
to Marley, Mutabaruka,
Madiba, Maya
Visions so bright led the
jailer to see he
twice imprisoned in
imprisoning another
behind the walls of
money is fair is right
wronged by the poor
in vibes in meditation
We shall all have money
when we see that honey
is not made for man
but for the bee family
from the sense of purpose
sense of tomorrow
is made from yesterday
Today is the now
How good and how
pleasant it is to be
a bee to be
good and pleasant

to those who are good
and pleasant
to the woman, child,
elderly, to brethren?
The peasant mind
that finds pleasure
to destroy, to maim
shall blame no one
for reciprocal demise
Twice is once too much
to fall to rise
beyond expectations
I man of the line of
conquerors slay every
dragon, cross every moat
I quote:
"In all things ye shall prosper."

Natty Dreadlocks Congo I

Natty Dreadlocks Congo I from Buzrack
Natty Dreadlocks Congo I will remain Black
Natty Dreadlocks Congo I get rejection
Natty Dreadlocks Congo I is still strong

See the Rasta Man
He remains the same
Not working for praise
Not working for fame
Never played that game
Still not tame
With his hair ragga ragga like lion's mane
Some say he is insane
Still Rasta's influence doesn't wane
Majestic work is not in vain

Natty Dreadlocks Congo I is no fad
Natty Dreadlocks Congo I teach simple lad
Natty Dreadlocks Congo I is a giant
Natty Dreadlocks Congo I work like bees, ants

Rastaman trod from a great distance
Constantly putting up resistance
I remember the Black Heart Man
It is no miracle the Wailers held us
The whole world listened
Still some remain in a trance
To murder music they continually dance
You remain strong Rasta
Bongo Man

Natty Dreadlocks Congo I step right
Natty Dreadlocks Congo I shine a light
Natty Dreadlocks Congo I build houses, many mansions
Natty Dreadlocks Congo I embrace I Africans

He says love right, reject wrong
Hail I, Binghi Man
Stand up!
Black redemption, reparations, repatriation
Blessed My Lord, Love I, Bobo Man
Get ancient facts from the voice box of the Orthodox
Don't watch critics, chant on ancient original Coptic
The Rastaman sound in country, in town
Rastaman sounds abound in all lands
I Izerve Rasta foundation stand strong
That is I Izervation of the Rastaman
The Natty Dreadlocks Congo I from Buzrack

In 1995 I approached Gussie Clark about producing this one and he suggested that I approach Mutabaruka to record it instead. I did not do that. "How dare he!?!" I thought. That is a decision I did, for a while, rue occasionally.

Have You Heard an N Word?

No doubt I am a house Nigga
who knows what you feel in the field Nigga
I suppose that makes me a feelin' Nigga
who sees a picture big, bigger than my pain
I am a feel Nigga who can push beyond
the fears that cripple
I am a feelin' Nigga who knows "the others"
we talk about aren't bad people ma Nigga
Different?
Yes, different
Your thoughts make them who they are in your mind
They too feel Nigga, but they focus on
a picture bigger than their bills, rent and mortgage Nigga
All people have a cause
What's yours?
What's mine?
What's ours?
I appeal to you brother man, sister chic so slick
There is plenty going on other than car payments
I pray thee, sister woman mister sleek
There is more to manhood than your biceps

No doubt I am an African born
in a land where my progenitors carried beyond
have survived horrors to be more than
dance moves, great kicks with a brand,
more than athleticism on a field
People are people being people
People will be people seeing differences in people
I tell you what's similar

Don't believe me test it
We are sets of habits
We are choosing to repeat
to self-defeat, collectively, repeatedly
Habits
We are cerebral tracks guided by feelings
Those who think they think more than those who feel
have not started to think beyond themselves

So, tell me ma Nigga,
tell me the N words that make you scared
makes you freeze when the light hits?
Is it noose? Is it night?
Is it negotiation?
Is it Neanderthal rising like water clouding over oceans?
What is the N word that scares you my Nigga?
Is it net worth or network?
I feel you ma Nigga
We can be bigger by choices
We can be new sets of habits…

Buoyant

Aren't we all in
the same boat
Cut the moorings
Let us shudder at
the weight of
the responsibility
of the rudder
Not harboured by
Our own thoughts…

Day After Michael Manley's Death

State of a fear of our own selves
Shelves fully stocked
Inventory of these islands
Centuries after identity eludes
Social costs greater than benefit
Jobs without benefits
"We're all dying
What will we give to mankind
before we venture into
the unknown?"
A fish for a dish
or a line for those who are
inclined to give of
knowledge they get?
What?
A net, a boat or means
to acquire both?

One Step

Men and people
it's supposed to
look plausible
while you fill your
crucible of blood
but it won't
From womb, light
Loom covers temple
Tomb accepts shell
What merit hath
free spirits?
What from these
souls go onto scrolls?
Scroll down this window
Surf these virtual spaces
Virtues, vices coexist
Co-create greater, yet
Net, lines given to big
fish who fish for small
fries to only bait who
cry to powers that be
all they want to be
except power for the
powerless…

African Forum – Ghanaian Drums

September Sunday morning
Smells of callaloo, plantain, eggs
Sunny side is the East
Sun's rays spray cirrus streaks
across blue canopy
Sleeping half-moon camouflages
with the cirrocumulus
Clouds are lifted from the inner
vision as the nightingales' songs
praise the now
Two doves perch on powerless
powerlines
In love
Myriad other bird songs
so powerful
My brother's birthday
Kwame Nkrumah's birthday
Ka'Bu Ma'at Kheru hammers
anvil of my ears with
songs from Accra
with WEB Dubois' Ghana Calling,
with Langston Hughes'
Manifesto for the Black Poet
How can I be quiet?
How can I deny these tears I cry?
How can I speak in jest?
I am blessed
PANAFEST a reality
Sister P, Sister Parchy
Spirituality…

I walk the blood soaked
dungeons of Elmina
Yes, with the bare feet of Mutabaruka
I walked on centuries of
my own hardened blood
Oneness
Every drum of Africa
plays in my heart
The first drum beats
to its own rhythm
The Rhythm of Creation

July 23, 1996

Nightfall
Birds are making
their various calls
Incandescent
Fluorescent
They come on with
various degrees
of fossil fuel glow
Half moon
hangs above
Metallic traffic
in concrete maze
Fleetingly pen
touches page
Open the door
Let in the sage
Musing, perusing,
choosing mind
Effusing heart
Letters, words
joining, coining
another song,
another praise
Nightfall
Insects sounds
drowned by various
combination of
urban sounds
Ants scurry by
taking food

to their nests,
their mounds
Should one say
this is just another
night that wouldn't
be entirely right
Tonight, I am one
with all Creation
In this aloneness
there's much company
All things, everyone
so near
Alone
I am away from me
All people are
who they are,
Alone I am me

Black Presence

I will not be Black History
until I make a history
that will help to shape
the future of Africans
in positive ways
Thought for a while
about where I am at
Blameless I am not
Acceptance not of what
clearly is not my lot
Blaming no one
for any situation
for my present coordinates
Acceptance of
my duties, responsibilities
Youth searched
for role models
found models playing roles
of machismo in the midst
of harsh economic realities
Inflated ego gets zero
of self's true state
My present state
is my own and no other's
So, what if there are snares?
So, what if slick foxes
are out of lairs
He who cares prepares
True, the image seen
on screens can affect esteem

For we have been trained
indoctrinated to be someone
outside ourselves
Trained to climb ladders
not our own
It is a hair-raising ride
going opposite direction
of this treadmill, this escalator
Hold on steady, strategize
Organize realize
ability's highest state

Philharmonic

I was in the band
Not as a player
As an instrument
Strung along
Taut stringed
instrument of
pleasure
Expertly plucked
Minstrels sang
Soothing sounds
Ocean's calming
ebb
Strength ebbs
Lullaby
Gullible I
Like baby's dribble
Comforting
Discomfort, curt
eventually — hurts
Allay then create
fears, fictional
Innuendo
Wait, tomorrow
Promises
Deafening
Crescendo…
Awake repeating
Not those mistakes

It Ain't Right to Fight

I am gonna say going to
I wanna say want to
when I am retired and have
enough of me just for myself
to say as I please
Then again, what difference does
it make if this ain't my language
or whether ain't is not a word?
Who cares?
I have done enough of
shapeshifting, fitting into roles
scripted, directed, reviewed
only to wind up here
just beyond where I started
thirty years ago dancing
with this same awkwardness
simply to get paid so we
all get laid across bridge's abutment
I can and I will do it again
with lessons added upon
Get laid, get paid
Get laid out for another's plans
Best laid plans for how to
smile, shuffle some more
from Black Pete to Black Street's
Diggity, more diggity
What is diggity anyway?
To know diggity will define
what is "no diggity"
But if you have to define it

diggity ain't for you anyway
For who gets to tell you, tell me
definition of words we invented,
words incorporated into vocabulary
that is not mine in the first place?
Place more emphasis on this syllable
Say it like you mean it
As we bleep out the N word
While the child says
Momma, with an accent not of
her Caribbean roots which is
not of Ghanaian coast or some other space
 from where her father's mother's
father's mother's father was shipped
as bookkeeper's statistic on balance sheet
insured by old, cold money,
bold money passed down
as we get over it because
we weren't there we simply inherit
inherited tendencies to find ways
to keep it
The money simply came with it
I am keeping it
Comfy fireplaces
It is not about money
It is not about colour
Jesus is white all right!
I wanna say want to
I am going to say gonna...
Momma, there is one too many Gs
In the N word and Mr. Okonkwo
Says the word is pronounced Niger

The first syllable they got it right
but second is pronounced like jeer
Are they jeering us momma?
Mr. Ugochukwu said it started as word of those
almost educated
The word's Spanish, but how could
we expect man whose best skill
was wielding whip to know Spanish
if the poor fellow was not even schooled in
English the language of his boss in the first place?
And momma my cousin Dantae says it is ok to start
a sentence with and, and any other word
I choose to because his oldest brother
was sentenced for saying nothing
about what he knew and his crew
says he is their real Nigga, so they take
care of his momma and all his siblings
He said the prison is really a corporation
He said I should tell no one, but
his cousin who went to the boogie school,
who wears ties with matching socks,
is a coon but he has a thing
called a philosophy that makes sense
He says his friends who aren't Niggaz
can call him a Nigga if they can spell Shaniqua
and keep a straight face while she comes
and clenches his neck with her thighs
He wouldn't say where she was coming from
but he says if she has his baby that
baby is gonna be a Nigga no matter
who is the father,
Momma, he says

45

in three generations you could never
tell that that Nigga's grandfather
was from northern Europe
He said sometimes
his cousin with the ties and socks talks silly that
everyone is from Africa but snow
changed their colours over time
He said forgiveness is for the strong,
that we should forgive them
they know what they did, know what they
do now, yet do it anyway
because it profits many fine people
finely clothed in apparel's finest
So fine catwalks don't see them
He said, she said, he said it's ok by him
even if they call his name as long as
they place emphasis on syllables correctly
Then he looked pensive with faraway
eyes seeing things that ain't there
He said he knows nothing about anything
He says real Nigga says
he ain't know nothin' and ain't saying
nothin' to nobody 'cause since double negatives
are wrong in sentences and Niggaz
can be sentenced for saying nothin'
when he ain't know nothin'
he ain't following no language rules
As for me, I want to say wanna and not be judged,
labeled, stereotyped right now
I wanna say what I have to say
I am gonna do what I must
to keep that right

I ain't gonna fight about it
That ain't nothing to fight about
It is mine
If fighting ain't right,
how is fighting for a right you
 were already born with right?
It seems, we may fight after all
But it ain't right and I don't wanna...

Just-Ice-Cold Stares

The only justice I have known
is poetic
My only defence against
polyethylene smiles
Your honour, my honour
is in my words, my actions
My lord let it be reflected
on the record that
I am licensed to kill
Poetic licence to kill
every wasp in my being
that will never be a bee
Honey is not made by money
Pollen is not stolen from flowers
Pollination is a nation's
duty to preserve for garden's sake
for children's fruit plates
The power of words
shall be felt by deaf, muted by none
If the detective is defective,
effective only when gun's cocked
let him be locked within
conscience's walls
The same sentence for unjust judges
It is my fate to free
psychological inmates
emancipate myself, brothers, sisters
in the poet's court
All rise!
Preside over your own fate

False pride, self-hate
shall not abide
Ride the underground-railroad
of knowledge

Addis Awaits More Creators

Said mother
There will be days like these
Rain will separate pollen from bees
That won't change the age of Geez
Grandma's wisdom has come with age
She has written much
Still, she turns new pages
She says wasps don't love bees
Wasps shirk, lurk, ambush, to sting
Bees rise, give praises
These are sunny days, work, sing
Grandpa spoke of Goliath
He spoke of Philistia's miscalculations
Told us he did of the shepherd's sling
Quietly he said:
Not even the dog that pisseth on the wall
Father won't rest until the work is done
His shoulder to the wheel
He counts not the clods
Tireless behind the plough
He knows there is a victory any day now
The pen is still mightier he says
Son, hang up the blade
But never blunt the cutting edge
Fearlessly walk through the valley
Rise for your prizes
Foundations are laid
Rome was not built in a day some will say
I say neither was Harare nor Addis Ababa

Breathe

Always shall a word as big as never guide me
Never shall a word as big as always leave me
Never shall I rest until those misguided enough
to label themselves my adversaries are vanquished,
put to shame by their own devices while I in silence
watch, breathe, breathe, in silence…

Breathe…

Never shall I unsheathe a sword caress a trigger

except in defense of this life,

for those it is my duty to protect

Never shall I cast aspersions on, look askance at another

Never shall I seek to justify any resentment

Never shall I raise the voice, clench these fists in anger

Never shall I compete with anything except my last standard

Never shall I seek to be seen, heard or understood

Never shall I explain my actions to the unimaginative

Never shall I be snared again by closed shallow minds

Always shall I be free from backbiting, gossip and guile

Always shall I be evolving beyond each new plateau

Slow, slower, slower yet…

Breathe…

Always shall I be vigilant, watchful at the gate of my mind
Always shall I repel every thought less than lofty about myself,
Always shall I invalidate every criticism of all detractors
for always shall this life be on the other side of the critic's slander
Always will I grow in places where shallow beings would be
drowned in even the thought of these depths

Breathe…

I came from nothing
I am no thing's thing seeking to be a thing among fleeting things
No thing, shall define me
Attached I am to nothing enough to be dragged by it
Fashioned by my own heart and mind I will prevail against
my thoughts of anything less than the best of who I am
For in this continuous journey, I am guided by my own stars,
my own charted courses
Always shall a word as big as never guide me
Never shall a word as big as always leave me
Never yielding always winning… Until the last breath,
I breathe…

Old Woman's Tale

Was speaking to older woman
We spoke about many things
She didn't want to be called ma'am
I had no time to wonder what
she was thinking
Such wisdom, profound voice
She kept talking
I kept listening
Her eyebrows had white hair
Lines on her face
told ancient stories
Found I couldn't leave
She spoke I listened
I asked questions
She answered
Then she asked one
Do you know where the wind
comes from?
If you know answer this question
You see trees sway
every single day
Where the wind comes from
no one can say
She spoke about Churchill
Told her I would prefer to
hear about Garvey
She paused
Did you know the man I asked?
She answered yes, proud, confident
The people did not understand

she said and those who did
feared him too much
They feared the people
Wise old woman
She spoke with me in my twenties
Let your main goal be to understand
Young man we are just travellers
Let your moments here count
Let it count for something
more than you
Be more than your ambitions

A Big City Tale

In a dog eat dog world
A lone dog
A determined dog
decided not to eat
Decided not to feast
not to cannibalize
An oddball
Soon he'll wither,
shrink, fall
They mocked,
they jeered
one and all
Without help
or words of endearment
alone without a bone
lone dog held his stance
Watched the feast
from a distance
Solitary canine
Why don't you join?
Come wine, dine
this meat is fine
'tis survival
We eat to live
We aren't cannibals
They did jeer
He's watching calories,
famished, abstaining
from niceties
Ravenous,

having nothing nutritious,
possesses nothing to
show some status
Lone dog branded
misfit
Sees many goals
knows he'll never quit
Learning lessons
late albeit
Wonders when they'll
feel the mystic
Wonders when they'll
get a hunch
There is no free lunch
In dog eats dog world

Exodus 34:13

"But ye shall
destroy their altars,
break their images
and cut down their groves"
Wait not at their firesides
Neither wait at their stoves
Plant your own vineyards
Take none of their herbs
Not even their spices
Play none of their games
regardless of variety
regardless of choices
Know HIM
Know The Christ
They took us to labour
in a strange land
on banks of rivers
similar to Babylon
Presented they onto us
many sideshows
multiple icons
Fast cars, fast food,
signs of neon
They did control tools
of manipulation
Mass communication,
constitutional writings
confusing with long sentences,
legal jargon
To players of instruments,

singers, writers of songs
they presented
financial considerations
They said play the music
with misleading words
so the children won't be
mindful of their fathers' lands
For the children were of
ancient traditions
Singers sang
Bands played on
Schools they built
from town to country,
childhood basic
through adult tertiary
Knowledge they gave
was not of self
Illusions presented
labelled they a privilege
Books they taught from
varied, plenty
Still they didn't teach
From books of Mr. Garvey
Neither his opinions
nor philosophy
Things they said about
the emperor Haile Selassie
caused the children
to forget HIM,
doubt his work
But even though they falter
It seems far too long

These children will go
to their fathers' lands
Restore the vineyards,
sing the songs
We shall not kneel at their altars,
We shall refuse their images
We shall plant our own groves

Friday Breeze

Elise,
I was cooled by an IRIE Evening Breeze
Now I am at a place Easy Skanking
I grow tall inside where roots buttress faith
I stand in the crowd alone in corporate maze
These are the days when I clear the haze

Silence...

Silence screams decibels
that conscience can't ignore
From the mountain of the soul there are
echoes across the valleys, across the plains
Climbed I to the peak where there are clear
views of splendid distant shore
I smile as ebb tide takes false pride
where they belong, away from this soul
to deep wide expanse where salty tears
become blue
Talking true to self
Listening
I'm not now wondering why
Linton Kwesi Johnson is wondering
Little wonder, that I wondered long
Why had I wandered away from me?
I wander no more
I from this mountain watched the shore
My feet, on dry land
Footprints there are on the beach
There is no sand on these knees

60

From where I stand
I see gulls fly to their nests
Behind the sun goes to rest
I stand and breeze plays on my face
There is joyful laughter in the leaves
These mountain trees...

Checked Luggage

Wary traveller am I
Never weary
Never jaded
Unbraided yet together
Apart yet a part of all
Waited not for paved surfaces
comfortable carriages
No companions
when speed is the need
never solo when distance calls
Wary
Aware
Self-awareness of self
being aware of self
being aware of self
in other selves
Wary
Perceptions examined,
mind parses, distils, owns
Soul owns in truths
accepts the world seen
within is not reality of all
if at all even reality itself
Self, self, self
says self-seeking only for self
Wary of those selves in selves only
Wary traveller
Wary of distances between
Wary of closeness
Wary of indifference, slights

Weary of those not wary
of their own self indulging
self-absorbed centre of world
complexes complicating simplest
straight lines from one point to
to parts known for attracting the wary…

Pathways

Different paths
have us all
We stumble, fall
Rise we must
Rise we shall
Different process
Slow progress
We meander,
digress, realign
Meandering streams,
gurgling brooks
All reach ocean's depth
All to cloud again
Cyclical us
We all rain
We glow us all
We grow, reproduce
Our thoughts,
feelings, stirrings,
strengths, foibles
All take us here
Take us where
we know we
must go
We conquer this
Inner space
We replace them
Habits that serve us not
We change
or be changed

Different paths
We trust, each of us will
trust our own process

Unpacking

She dated men
Waited tables of men
She hated men wearing ties,
Men who don't wear ties
Men with ties tied too long,
tied too short
Tied just right, written about in
manuals just for men
Tied in unconventional knots
Men who don't own ties
Men who tie them in front of mirrors
Tie them hurriedly while catching trains,
She baited men with
Bust line low, hem short
Legs crossing slowly
Panty-line showing, panty-less days
Subtle ways, suggestive plays
She didn't know her father
She looked for one in men greying
at the temples
working out in gyms,
overgrown paunches in sports bars
expensive restaurants,
trim from laps in pools,
making moves only those
in boardroom's circle of trust may
She always had another card to play
Men are pigs, dogs, hogs, beasts
Let them pay
Let them spoil their lives spoiling me

Break their routines,
change their good habits saving
damsel in manufactured distress,
tight fitting dress
She read men
Not like spellbinding books…
Books to be edited shredded
Rewritten
Smitten by her own devices,
She hated whores
They are too honest about sex
too generous to these men
They should pay for the idea
of sex happening in hotels, they pay
for in distant places where jets
aren't fast enough to reach soon enough
She hated dancers
who gave lap dance,
took their chances with strangers
Stranger are the things she imagines
She awaits men, who dare say,
"Hi, good day,"
Those especially opening doors
for wives like mom never got,
gestures she does not care for

She the controller of her destiny
flailed by her mirror daily
wears a smile practiced, perfected
But eyes do not lie
She hated men
especially those who love women

enough to not desire them all
She bears the fury of woman admired
Dead you are to her if you ignore her
Who dares scorn this carefully
adorned, accessorized package?
Who is he who does not speak the
lust languages?

Most intensely she hates men
who openly admire women,
men who dare tell her they do
How dare you look at me with admiration?
What do you want?
How dare you be attracted to feminine beauty?

Simply Because I Can

Stretched piano string taut
Wound up watch spring tight
yesterday, tomorrow, tonight
Self-mastery, the ideal sought
Caught in reveries ought not to be shared
Wings grow from these roots
of wind tested evergreens

Twing twang
Do, Re, Mi
For so long...
...then longer, yet
Tick, tock, locked into
grooves of
Jazz, Reggae, Calypso, Zouk
and more riding
upon waves' crests
moonbeam rhythms even tone deaf
while chiming bamboo winds
of mahogany glossed stillness
into weeping willow laughter

Left to own devices
vices trend
Virtues self-righteously
scoff at quests to grow,
ability to change, evolve
These controlled tear ducts seal
Medicine time
Laughing out loud from eyes

seeing beyond sight's impaired
intuition looks into the multi-dimensional
lines of blurred one dimension
of virtual make believe in
modernity's amnesia

Dissolved in Caribbean sweetness
washed upon salty shores
absolved by time's
ever patient trek to
ability's talented honing
these pens obey
I will this mind...
Go beyond writer's block

Simply because I can...

Smiling Chatter

I the talkative one talked until
they shouted me down with silent stares
My own words used to silence my voice's
squelched utterances babbling into state
of oblivion in town's square
encircled by siblings who did nothing
Out of nothing carved I mindset of
ocean's ebb tide hugging river's mountain
journey to estuary's salty freshness
crashing warm waters
into tropical iceberg mountains
I shall be voiced in places where eyes gleam
at voices' candid sounds of 'we are one'
We are apart being together for our own
sake of doing for you what I desire for me
I shall be told when I have told enough
which shall not be more than,
A smile…

Sound Bites

Non-linear, layered,
multidimensional we are
I am collection of sound bites
that have grown into chapters
I am more than status updates,
more than tweets
Birds shall twitter until well after dusk
When nightfall they shall appear
then they shall hoot
Let the feathered ones be grounded
if they are ostriches, emus,
turkeys, domesticated fowls
Let each scowl be converted
over time into smiles
Let there be windfalls
for all who toil, those who hustle, who grind
Let us be reminded of our connectedness,
our symbiotic inextricable bonds
Let us go beyond the limits of
our present vocabulary
Give depth to our expressions,
breadth to our reach
Not preaching, not teaching, just being
If we shall reach even one
If we are an example to another
We have lived for a purpose...

Children Are Not Annoying

A child smiling anywhere
is a child smiling
A child crying anywhere
is a child crying

You don't know who is
my father?
Not you, him!
You don't know why
I didn't go to school today?
To come here and distract me
from my work
No, to see the doctor
I can't go to school with cold
Go over to daddy's office
No!
Be quiet then, ok?
Yes
Three perhaps four minutes after
tiny hands covered my eyes
A whisper, another inquiry
You don't know when
is my birthday?
Today?
No
Tomorrow?
Cupped my ears, whispered
After Christmas
Don't tell him yu nuh!
Little girl smiles

especially her eyes
At crowded Times Square
bus station
Japanese toddler's tantrum
washed his mother with tears
Real tears
Real tears from child on
overcrowded Kingston bus
Child cries for bag juice
Mother's eyes looked
at distant place with
eyes that had seen
eyes that had shed tears
Tears my heart into tiny pieces

A Pause for Bigger Applause

The artless have made an art
of stealing art from the artistic
Artful
Heart full of hurt
Out of dirt comes diamonds
Shining, cutting, diamond
Some laughed at the coal
Couldn't see the goals
Gold glitters
Plastic, smiles now metallic
Idyllic
Poetic
Forsake not the cause
for temporary applause

Knock Knock

I hear some say heaven is
above, way up in the skies
beyond highest clouds
above golden moon, sun,
stars, distant galaxies
One night in silence
I knocked heaven's door
I knocked heaven's door
Heard inner answers
These heartical emotions
balanced truths within
The heavens declare wonders
Silence
The conscience's freedom
Patience for knowledge's sake
Application is the power
Innerstanding
Wisdom of ages
Pages for sages
Cages are open for words
declaring wonders within

Daylight

Left in the dark
With a little spark
Stark naked
Stripped of dignity
In identity's crisis
I cried
When came fear
there was feeling
to cry for help
to be led back
to their light
there mirror shows
Ego said go
to old familiar
not knowing
how close it
was to daylight

Laugh Out Loud

Sometimes I cry
Sometimes I cry
Sometimes I cry so hard
no sound comes from my lips
I cry so hard the floor
gets slippery
I cry from a place where
most are afraid to visit within
I cry so hard my eyes sting
then see so clearly
That is when I laugh most freely
I laugh so freely
My mind thinks so clearly
Solutions appear
Sometimes I cry
Because I have to sing
Because I have to love
I cry
I cry as only a poem can
Cry for cowards who fight
Cry for those who take flight
Cry for those who
think they cannot
Cry with those who
know they must
For those who trust
processes, work, wait
For those who know
it is and will be all right
We cry together

We cry hard
We laugh even harder
Oh, what joy it is
to be joyful for joy's sake

Swords vs Pen Points

There shall be no swan songs
Neither will there be Parthian shots
Haves say they have not for have nots
Have nots have the power to have what
they have not made up their minds yet
to go out and get
Haves have not the desire to have
have nots empowered, enlightened
not frightened by their own radiance
I have not time
It is not mine to waste on fighting
I shall sing songs of my heart daily
Away from condescending ears
Near banks of rivers of my ancestors
It has been a while since
I sat on banks of the Nile
The banks of these rivers are cold
Only the bold ones' quiver is full
Only there bowstrings still not taut
See them stand arrayed militant
Word warriors armed with their pens

Interdependent

Behind the eyes of storms
are tempestuous times
Calm is inevitable
Troubles aren't forever
Behind these eyes are tears
that will not be shed before
eyes that cannot see that
these aren't tears of fear
Ears can't hear what ought
to be heard
Fly uncaged bird fly freely
Sing songs of redemption
I think I know why Maya's
bird sings
Its quest is to rest in a nest
made of straws gathered
with its own efforts

Mirror

Sick?
Of Me?
Mirror in my face
who is the sickest
of us all?
Hic! Hic!
In your face I see
me sparkling in
eyes beholding me
I hear from lips
saying only the
best about me
Sick of me?
I'll give you
a cure
More of me...

Neighbourly

My neighbour, so hard
to reach it seems
Prisoners we appear to be
Zoo animals in metal cages
The burglar's bar of rage
screams down barrel of a gun
In every zinc fenced
or gentrified space
We seem so apart
together on this tiny island
Corporate success seems elusive
We appear to be slipping
through a sieve
The guns will have to stop
Dogs will bark
Barrels of crabs
that are perceived
will be what they are in time,
Just perceptions
We will communicate
We will win
African people will win…

Beings Being Beings

Being a being being being
I be
Beings being beings for being beings
they have to be
Not just a being
A just being justified in being
who knows just what
it takes to be
Beings being beings be for
the sake of being beings
The state of being is
being being
Be between being because
being is what being shall be
Be belittled by no other being
Be believer of no other being's
beliefs that is not of your being
Be beautiful for beauty's sake,
being beautiful
Be beknown for being a being
who is being all
that you are capable of being
says enlightened beings
Beings being beings be
That is all there is to being being,
Being…

Shepherd Arrives

I urge myself to purge until
ego can be picked up with tweezers
Purge until every crowd pleaser
learns from my action that it is
much easier to be a man
My habits cannot be worn by nuns
Melanin skinned brother be pure
for the sisters of Nubia
I urge myself to purge until
There is an upsurge of energy
that makes every dirge into
a song of joy, a song of praise
Purge until spiritual heights make
me lighter than angels
until I get off my knees
Purge until there is no space
to brag
The money bag sags because
the city is hazy not because
people are lazy
We cannot be bogged
Smog will clear when we have
left city's plains
We gain more than status symbols
I have my head in the clouds
for I dwell in mountain space
where no trace of city pace invades
sanctum of innerstanding
Higher I dwell than marshland
Land of ancient man ancient woman

85

rescues telepathically
Empathetic are truths
seeking not alliances partnerships
Empathetic and silent
So silent that conscience makes
insomniacs writers of lullabies
Sleep not near wolf packs
Weep not for innocent sheep will
come home
The gullible will be stronger when
they learn to beware of smiles
from lips lies behind eyes

Ego

Ego
Self-thinking subject
I am the object of all
that transpires around me
Ego must let go
Give a chance to dance
Getting out of the picture
Allow mind, soul to soar
Ego shall let go
Ego shall be bruise-proof
Watch me take some time
to roll in simplicity
Watch me respect fellow beings
expecting not to be respected
Watch me give not to get
Fewer to zero are regrets
Ego, let go
Ego I let you go to
voicemail
Talk with you later...

Silence

Silence
Oh faithful companion
Encircle me
Silence
Oh unpredictable friend
Never leave me alone
When impulses rage
Lock this tongue
Seal these lips
Let not one word
from them slip
Silence
So keen on observation
Stay with me when
words crowd my head
seeking an outlet
When anger rages
speech may bring regrets
Silence rule over me
Faithful sun
Reflecting moon
Never late, never soon
Rising setting in silence
Economy of words
Precision
Soul words
Every breath counting
Every sound
Then, silence
Rejuvenating moments

of healing, reflection
Meditation, prayers
All questions, all answers
in silence…

Contemplative

If for a fleeting moment
I had stopped to listen
given myself a chance
to hear instead of being
heard by you
If for future fleeting
moments
I remain silent
you will feel the arrow
not knowing the bow
was bent
Then I'll watch you flutter
My double pleasure the word
that was not uttered
the fact that you did not know
contents of my quiver
If for a fleeting moment
I remain silent...

Thankfully I keep talking...

Dis Mek Sense?

Sat they there
Saturday morning
Satideh mawnin
Some idrin
Half Way Tree
a reason like
dem a quarrel bout dis
Dis nuh rispeck no one
Who dis who
Bout disrispeck
Disrispeck nevah
expeck fi si knife draw,
stone, mashiate
One seh him did
have a slug
So I jus journey faahwud
to I bug grab I book
I dicshaneri
Proactive livity
Haawt an head work
complimentary
Dis Rhyme is very, very,
very me, si me livin
pan dis rock wid
I idrin, I sistrin
Livin wid I woman
an chile
Once upon a time
long aftah stories
did begin wid once upon a time,

91

I would cry fi I people,
how dem laas dem vibes
I eye could nevah stay dry
Jus do what I
have to do
For whom all who
I can for as long as
I can I will, I shall…

Breath of Life

Breath of Life
Let me be thankful
first for the ability
to be thankful that
I will always be
thankful for being
able to be thankful
for the giving of
thanks
I pray that I will
never be predator
or prey
That I will always
be prayerful
praying for prayers
that make me pray
more but do even
more of what I
pray for
I will always try
to make my actions
reflect my prayers
that I will always
act first to seek
springs to quench
my thirsts
Not bearing weights
of waiting for
a miracle
That I will always be

mindful of the miracle
that I am
I am miraculous
A promise of what the
future holds living in
the present guided by
my past
My past shines lights
in my paths
My shadow shadows
no one
A beacon I am
I am a lighthouse
a reference point,
a benchmark
Judge me by whatever
standard that you
choose for my standards
are shifting, lifting me up
beyond my comfort zone
honing my blade
whetting the edge
shaping the hedge
weighting the sledge
that breaks boulders
in my path
My wrath is temporary
Constant is my joy
Postponed is pleasure
of gratification's impulse
Gradually, gracefully
surrendering youth

Fiction of Time

Celestial realms of time
Time ever changing, elapsing
leaving moments in chronicles,
archives of events, lives
Every passing moment
Every moment called now
Every chime
Every grain of sand falling
through narrow glass space,
counted on lunar, solar charts
Every tick on precision instruments
Every moment preceded by, followed
by moments called now
Now we occupy this space
In this place, that place
Space, place in cyclic journeys
On Earth
Mother Earth
Mother Earth gestating,
constantly producing
fruits for man's insatiable
want, our needs, greed
Man's quest to maintain
speed in life's fast lanes
Our short journey, our ride
Mother Earth malleable,
Pliant
Never refusing when man
excavates even for the sake
of hate

95

Mother Earth
She always reclaims her own
All remains here on this plane
If not here, some other place
Would that man could save time
locked away in vaults
Would that man could loan time
like he does money
with interest then some would
only a generation live
Had man power to manipulate time
like pawns protecting kings
in life's chess games
Power play of less work, more gain
More work more pain, less tangible gains
for those blamed of being lazy
Is it good that man cannot
manipulate time?
Good that man cannot
make a maze of time,
twist then unravel through reason
through logic,
exercises of intellect, of wit
Good that ephemeral,
perennial time is no well-used cliché,
metaphor, rhetoric
Great, it is never late
There's always a moment,
Now

A Part of Our Story

Stop think for a while
about our glorious past
on the banks of the Nile
Man if you are mindful
of my scowl you can
appreciate my smile
Should you wonder
why my poem has
no refrain, no catchy
punchline, no chorus
chances are you aren't
aware that our story was
once written on papyrus
once free from computer
virus
Should you marvel at
today's seemingly novel
inventions
Then you might not have
heard words from Ethiopia,
Abyssinia, Nubia
Words from Mali, from
Egyptian historians
Indeed civilizations are
many that my story spans
Man is beyond extinction
I African has been, will be
for centuries to come
One needs not be marvelled
All things have been since

the earth's been peopled
Of depth, skin and beauty
Consider Akhenaten,
Nefertiti
Man dates older,
before them
What questions ask us
therefore, of what shall be
has been before?
Man's super ego sits on
tactless, unsubtle, indelicate,
uncompromising foundations
of truths
So Freud can never fill
my spiritual voids
Multi-faceted mankind
It is now
The moment now
Never clichéd
Never say never some say
Ask I may of smart, of clever
Say never say never without
saying never

Heal this Heel

Jamaica's Achilles heel
Skin of my skin
Kin of my kin
Of darker tint
Of lighter hue
Of different class, caste
Sharing similar future
Sharing different pasts
Presently building
sandcastles in hurricanes
for no national reasons
It is so hard for this
wonderful nation to stand
on tired feet
We all know it is not true
that only a certain hue
must fetch or hew
for a few who chew
more than they can digest
A few who out of many
extract much
Much is given to whom
much is expected
yet much more is taken
when self is forsaken
to feel beholden to
another for morsels
Collectively we limp
along singing Redemption Songs
to redeem the psychologically

unjust who must enslave
another to feel complete
Dip us all in objectivity
Towel us dry with open-mindedness
Clothe us with tolerance, empathy
Clothe us with patience
Atlantic slave trade makes
most people ashamed to speak
but it is time to unpack
that rickety old vessel

State of Sobriety

Said preacher man on radio
"Old pirate turned planter
turned merchant
turned members of the
North St. Andrew caucus
have once again moved
to secure their power base."

Days after
Police channels officially
said he in Buckfield of unsound mind
attacked police with stones, with knife
Police fired in defence
Pronounced they he at hospital, dead
Amateur video footage
showed beating with baton
On ground defenceless
Without weapon
Voice of woman said
"Light him up!"
Trigger squeezed by police
Man writhed
Extra judicial
Statistic
Ballistic
Hic, hic, hic
Kilometres away
All-inclusive insulates
Alcohol obliterates
Party time, state crime

Party time gyal wine, artiste says
Show yuh navel ring, tongue ring, show yuh tattoo
Live some life while yuh young
Long weekend
What's there to do?
Give some more to the few
The few...

Old pirate turned planter
turned merchant
turned philanthropic ventriloquist
moves subtle as chameleon
from downtown to the villages
with message of
borrow more, spend responsibly
Longest liver is the designated driver
Drunk on political rhetoric
teetotaller with healthy liver educated mind
searches for jobs, more jobs
Wonders which people are put first
Collective thirst for vinegar
Fermented cane goes East
For sugar came we to these shores
As thick as molasses
our ancestors' blood poured into irrigation canals
Tea time, afternoon siesta
More sugar, less cream
Kowtow, smile, shuffle
Now is the time
Time is right
Smoke signal, drum message turned
text message, turned email, instant message

Message in a bottle alcohol volume
increases, challenges manhood

Emancipation Day broadcaster in Ocho Rios said,
"We must be very clear in our minds
about the significance of this day, this freedom
that we celebrate…
We must become our ancestors."

New Blighty

Mighty island of North Sea to Atlantic
Smitten you have been by power
Written you have stories of gain
Always the conqueror
Strong I know you are
Mighty conqueror of distant shores
Planting flags mighty island of conquest
Uprooting ancient landmarks
Displacing weak, vulnerable, gullible
Replacing shame with greater shame
Great your claim mighty island across
channel from mainland of your kindred
of languages different, oh how tired you must be
Oh how battle scarred you are mighty one
From Northern Nordic losses you've gained
From Roman servitude you have broken bondages
From fascist tyranny you have freed your brethren
returned dignity to your sisters of your hue
even while you return to old familiar places
labelling me not your kin for my skin's sake
Whither your centuries houses of paper
your sandcastles?
Why have you been so scared of hunger
even while your granaries overflow?
Why so afraid of thirst even while wells
sunk so deep regenerate and flow perpetually?
We have seen you mighty one
You have put to sword
You have divided in ways that left Machiavellian
manoeuvres fit for sainthood

Surely you must be tired old friend
With your steely grip on throats of servant class
With hounds baying at your fox-like balance sheets
You seasoned hunter playing prey
crying victimhood, even
you must be weary of wariness of all
When will you rest from wolverine ploys
in sheep herd?
How will you rest in bed of radioactivity?
When will you outrun your tail you chase?
When will you visit Caribbean shores
with dignity befitting well-polished
highly burnished close to truths yarns
aligning with your actions?
For you have been labelled bitch,
hardboiled in cauldrons of enmity
slow cooked into sauces not even you can savour
You have been labelled bitch
but I say you are a woman of dignity
You shall live that calibre, that ilk with graciousness
For if you were such then we of Caribbean surrogacy
would be but flea bitten pups in your kennels
Oh woman of dignity
Oh man of noble intentions
Pave a road to heaven wherever you
consider that to be
Welcome yourself into the human family
Rest from your conquests
Take a break from your bondage
Let your lifelong guarding of prisons
be evolved into the nurturing of gardens,
Forging of plough shears

Let ears of corn grow from your minefields
Let binary ciphers wrap around
the reparations you so long to pay
to your African family members

This Poem Continues

These poems which is this poem
are inspired by *This Poem* which is
written by Mutabaruka
These poems were written on
papyrus in Kemet
These poems were written in
hieroglyphs, in Geez from Kush,
Alkebulan
These poems tell about Axum,
Lalibella, Songhai, Calabar, Mali,
Ghana, Akan, Dogon, Ibo, Yoruba,
Mandingo, Asante, Kikuyu
They tell of all people of Africa
Tales of civilization becoming,
unfolding, then folding up again
like petals shy wilted
These poems were written in
Timbuktu
Theses, precis upon precis
were taken from these poems
From Salamanca to UWI Mona,
St. Augustine, Cave Hill
to Oxford, Cambridge, Yale
Every fraternity claim these poems
These poems take no side,
have nothing to protect, to hide
These poems are being told
in secret by greying men
who now wonder how could
children be reciting these poems

These poems are geriatric crimes
Nursery rhymes, lullaby chimes
drowned out by exploding bombs
killing Walter Rodney but spreading
his message deeper long after
the sound subsides
These poems are young people
sent by disagreeing old people
to get their PTSD continually
reaching for a phantom limb
These poems are amputated
by unsterilized legislations
These poems regenerate from
gangrenous stubs in kindergarten
doodles
Poodles mate with monsters
producing hybrids that fiercely
protect these poems
These poems need no protection from implosion
These poems are faithful pens
uncompromisingly urging insomniacs
write right, right where you left off
when fear crippled your mind
Right wrongs of Africans in the
Diaspora selling Africans further down
deep rivers for shallow gains securing
pay checks that secure them only close to
or until the next pay check
These poems secure everyone who secure
the now with yesterday's lessons
These poems need no security
As fleeting as mist, as desert sand blown

s lasting as mountains are these poems
Vaults are filled with these poems
Filled with paper, with engravers' ink, with ores
dug up, processed from these poems
by people trying to ignore these poems
Spreadsheets cannot cover these poems
Teraflops cannot process these poems
Terabytes cannot tell all about these poems
that have been written before keyboards
were invented
There will always be writers of these poems
These poems will choose them
They cannot run, will not be able to hide
from these poems
Everywhere they go these poems will be
waiting, showing them reasons for writing
These poems shall urge, demand and get
reparations for Atlantic trade in Africans
enslaved but still singing these poems
The writers of these poems shall not be afraid
to be labelled
Lazy minds shall find these poems
confusing, complex, tense
Oppressors shall pay to hear these poems
for these poems will give them conscience
These poems will free the brave
A truth about these poems is that these poems
will not claim to be the truth about anything
These poems are just words meeting
truths along conscience's journeys
Truths guide these words
Now

First Kabul Full Moon

Mother Moon
Night before your full face shows
I stand on mountain high
So close to you
Your ways never have I tried to know
I simply accept you Mother
If I were a wolf tonight I would bay
Howl I would
So fraught with danger these mountains
So accustomed they are to human pains
Mother Moon so near I am tonight
Somehow you seem to tell me more
near the shores though Mother
What are you saying in oceans tonight?
Dearest Mother,
what flotsam drift in your sway?
What lagoon Mother Moon shimmers your beam?
What seafarer hopes to make it
safely to bay, to harbour?
I would bay at your brilliance
if I knew that language
Mother Moon how silently you give
Mother Moon though city lights
induce oblivion to your presence
you show your face
Rock my boat Mother
Sing me a song of oceans deep…
Weep not oh Mother, I know you won't
Sleep – Oh no Mother you have not,
Mother Moon…

Mountain Shores

All rivers eventually flow
to mighty ocean no matter
how winding their paths
Have your day
Be satisfied with the bounty
of your heart
Let wisdom be sought by the
simple,
Let joy be with all
Let the ears of those who
seek to be in the presence
of those without guile, hear
Let those with faults cast
stones on houses of glass
We all reign
Subjects we all are
Let he who has humbled
himself be subjected to none
with vain thoughts masked
behind rituals
Let those without guile walk
not in paths of those deceptive
Speak life says the man
Let none saying "aha!"to their kit,
to their kin be satisfied in
their judgemental eyes
Let all who seek the welfare
of another be satisfied
Not every flower attracts bees
Every caterpillar cocooning shall fly

We the bearers of light chase
not deceivers into
darkened spaces
We know who we are
We are relieved to be freed
from entangling webs of duplicity
We are satisfied
We live...

We live...

Afghan Sojourn

As man's affection towards his brother
does not belie his strength
woman's beauty is not covered by hijab
Upon this mountain, strength I have seen,
incomparable beauty unhidden
When snow covered hills melt before Nowruz,
trees bud leaves, birds give praises for
skies blue unclouded
I have seen your heart felt your joys
Stronger than your pains are your
hospitable ways
Longer than each generation's journey
are your traditions
Under Afghan full moons have I carpeted
this space with yearnings for your peace,
This place of reflection remains with me
When shall I return free to roam, to wander?
I am but sojourner in your land
Temporary as wind moving sand
To me what gifts have you not already given?
For friendship, hospitality, acceptance
on this mountain, I am grateful...
Let my gratitude be etched upon a stone

Let it be written in the hearts
of each Afghan I meet
Say my name to your grandchildren
Speak of me...
Speak of that which I did overcome
while in your midst

Before I journey home, speak of flaws
in me that you see
Of any virtue you may have encountered,
Say it to another sojourner in your land
If for only one moment fleeting, ephemeral
you remember me with a smile,
anything else, a bonus shall it be
For we have broken bread,
We have spoken from hearts,
expressed ideas from heads
When from this mountain strong
I have departed, mention my name
Then I shall say to you,
Friend...
You are my friend
Khair Bebeenee shall be on my lips
In island space I shall recall you
Strong...
Strong as Hindu Kush range

You have rearranged my thoughts about you
Afghanistan shall my voice say (with ghayn)
To all who shall listen
they will hear me say,
Tashakur
Zhwand!

Red Rose

Touch not the rose
If you're not wary of thorns
Keep out of gardens
If manure you scorn
Keep on paved spaces
Buttons, belt, gib-line,
straightened laces
Look into honourable
eyes of those with burnt faces
We are going places
we've never been before
Holding no grudges
Settling no scores
We are of strong folks
tribes, resilient clans
As for I butterfly
I was born a caterpillar
Never the space filler
On journeys to places
I belong even though
I may not even know
they exist
Come let's go to Accra
One stop in Calabar
Prairie lions, mountain climbers
We love, we care our gardens
Rose with thorns will do us
no harm, no hurt, no pain
Delicate orchids
Begging no pardon

of those with hearts
so hardened
For this is a softer space
Reflective place of beauty
Beauty knows her duty
cares for more than skin's
glow, its hue, its texture
Show us paths leading
to places with little, no wrath
If by chance we should
stop where bedlam reigns,
Give us solace in the aftermath
So, touch not beautiful rose
if you thumb your nose,
judge by clothes,
shiny baubles,
practiced poses
For those who care
with pruning shears,
Those who take time to listen
Those who do hear
Those who support
Those who push past fears
Those who care even when
no one shows gratitude
They shall sleep well
They shall be rewarded

Emergency Landing

Under bus fast moving
Thrown to be crushed
Neglected, ejected, rejected
Scorned, derided, pilloried
What gifts brought they
What grist for mills
What skills obstacles did build
Grateful vessel
Fateful lessons
Stripped, whipped,
Ill-equipped for journey
Retooled then fooled the fool
who schooled the jewel, the gem
in ways of servitude
With new attitude,
excellence rose to surface
With pluck, grit, fortitude
dug foundations deeper
Keeper of no man's secrets
of horrors, tales of conquest
Gas-lit, snipped, cut, pasted
in another's script
by passive aggressive,
double chinned, cheek jowl
foul minded complex
Blindsided, double crossed
Slick micro aggression, veiled
nuanced moves of puerility
Transparent to intuition
Play me a dub session

for I have grooves for days
Days like these, fly I way up
above where ego starves
for oxygen's breaths
No attention
Attention spans better chasms
For all this is but launching pad
Runways for brave people...

Up where air is rarefied
Flew this craft with passengers
safe from judgemental piercing
stares of hatred
Deeper we fly into inner space
place where only each can know
Far away from man from Lansing
dancing to instruments not in song
Strong enough for heights
Skilled enough for landing anywhere
Always those grounded
shall get home
Even where there's no runway
we shall be safe
In their familiar beds
Tonight, rest these passengers
Safer than Sully on the Hudson
Landing
Innerstanding
Landing even on mountain,
upon cape
Not hidden from radar
No desperate measures

These treasures
Not too near to be far
From petty sandboxes
Landing even on jetty
Born with wings
Born with deep roots
Nothing keeps me shadowed
Or up in the sky…

Made in the USA
Middletown, DE
30 May 2021